Janey Mac Goes to War

Janey Mac Goes to War

Janey Mac Goes to War
ISBN 978 1 76041 432 0
Copyright © text Janey Mac 2017
Cover art: Abbas Diba
Cover design: Janey Mac

First published 2017 by
Ginninderra Press
PO Box 3461 Port Adelaide 5015 Australia
www.ginninderrapress.com.au

Contents

Gallipoli 2015 #1	7
The Real War	8
Endgame #1	14
And Who Shall Fight the Peace?	15
The Cliché: How It Starts, How It Ends	18
Just Another Cynical War Story	20
aside	29
You Leave Tomorrow	30
Analysis	32
A la Recherche du Guerres Perdues	34
Endgame #2	40
A Hundred Years From Now In Both Directions	41
Gallipoli 2015 #2	44
A War That's Not A War	45
Kite	46
A la Recherché du Guerres Perdues (Part 2)	47
Endgame #3	52
What it means	54
Western haiku	55
Bury the Dead	56
Blindsided: A Song of Innocence and Experience	64
Time's up	69
Lest we forget	70
The New Possibility	72
Do Not Confuse Life With Illusion	78
Endgame #5	79

Gallipoli 2015 #1

Dawn.
Fifteen thousand sand-eyed trippers
waiting for the holiday sun to rise
where history never will.
Ghosts of strangers' memories
hover in hearsay tableaux
of imagined heroics as a lone
bugler spits plaintive brass
over complicit grief.

Down at the front, old farts in seats shuffle and weep
while, back at the bus, beached backpacks
stuffed with sentiment and Speedos,
condoms, Bundy and third-rate grass
from Istanbul lie mounded in quick heaps.
Shit, it's cold – but there'll be a hell of a party here tonight.

The Real War

As soon as he walked into the café, he saw the girl. She sat towards the back, away from the boarded-up windows, holding a cup of steaming black coffee between her hands. Like everyone else in what was left of the town, she wore the scars of her survival with acceptance; covered in grime, the backs of her delicate hands were scratched blue with ingrained dirt and bruising; her cheeks and forehead were smudged grey; the rags she wore for clothes were caked with the filth of countless unwashed days.

But still she was beautiful. Enough to draw the eye of any observer. Her hair, badly cut and half hidden beneath a scarf that might once have been red, shone blue-black even in the joyless gloom of the unlit café so that it looked as though some hidden light played on it. And its brilliance was matched by that of her downcast eyes. Also black, with the depth of dignity in them which comes only in the transcending of poverty and hopelessness.

The soldier stood in the doorway, his gaze fixed on the girl. During his time in the army, he had seen many girls and many women; he had seen his comrades with them, taking them one after another, using them and discarding them; old women, their looks gone, their spirit broken, lying in the rubble while the conquering forces laughed above them, dribbling drunken spit onto their faces as they were repeatedly degraded and abused; young girls, not yet past puberty, prized by gangs of six or eight at a time, held whimpering while their liberators took turns – again and again – to exact full payment for their liberation.

Yes, the soldier had seen much even if he shunned the taking part in what he saw. But he had never seen anyone like this girl drinking cheap coffee in a bombed out café.

'What d'you want?' the sweating man behind the counter demanded, tossing a dirty cloth onto the bar top.

Startled from his trance, the soldier looked around him, glancing at the sullen hostile faces openly staring up at him. They were all covered with the tribal markings of the defeated: dirt, bandaged wounds, poverty, hunger. Above all, hunger. Despite his youth – the soldier had just turned twenty – he recognised the hunger he saw for what it truly was. More than the simple, pure hunger for food, it was the hunger for freedom from oppression, the hunger for release from fear. It was the essential hunger for life, however meagre.

'Coffee,' he said, his voice a practised command. And then, remembering the girl, he added, 'Please.'

He took the cracked cup to a table far from the door and far from the windows, to a position of considered safety. Even though the fighting was over here in this town, it paid to be careful. He sat facing the counter so that it looked as though he was watching the café owner. But in fact, from the corner of his eye he watched only the girl with the headscarf.

The coffee was vile, bitter and thick and flavoured with something far removed from what he remembered as coffee. But the soldier sipped it through gritted teeth knowing he would find nothing better anywhere in the town.

Outside, the day began to fade towards curfew and the café slowly started to empty until, with no more than minutes of the day left, only the girl and the soldier remained.

'Don't you know about the curfew?' the café owner growled. 'I've got to get halfway across town to go home. C'mon, out.'

For a second, the soldier seemed ready to respond with anger. He was used to more respect than this open contempt. But the girl was getting up, pushing away her cup, moving from the table, and he had to leave with her. With barely a glance at the owner, the soldier left the café, stepping into the cooling air of the street.

The girl was waiting for him, standing quietly at the kerb, her chin lifted in a challenge as he approached. Without a word, she turned and set off unhurrying along the street. A pace behind, the soldier followed.

'Where are we going?' he asked. 'Do you live nearby?'

The girl merely quickened her step but not too much. She seemed to be moving with the eagerness of anticipation rather than the desire to escape.

Behind her, the soldier's excitement grew as he watched her body in the subtle descending purple of the evening. She moved with a grace and sensuality he'd never seen in the frightened jerkings of those others, those who had submitted to the force of his comrades. For the first time since the war began, he thought he understood a little what the others felt.

The girl glanced over her shoulder, cast him a shy smile and lowered her eyes as she turned away again. They were in a part of town he hadn't seen before, a poor suburb badly damaged by the liberation. Craters gaped in the road and smoke drifted from occasional piles of rubble in the street. Houses without roofs, others missing a wall, were still home to families where children cried and dogs barked and lives were lived in full view of anyone passing. It would take more than a lifetime to rebuild the shattered lives around here, the soldier thought.

The air was thick with the congealing stink of recent artillery and too few cheap vegetables boiling in too much water. Suddenly gripped by shame and guilt, he wondered if he should pay the girl, leave her a few coins to ease her hardship. But before he could decide, she had turned into an alleyway between two derelict houses and he found he had to concentrate lest he lose her in the darkness.

At the end of the alley, she waited until he came close, until she could feel his breath on her face, and she reached out her hand to take his in a soft grasp. She put a finger of her other hand to his lips to check his voice. Ssh… Quietly, she led him through a doorway and into a passage cluttered with household wreckage, a stove, mangle, bedstead, all smashed beyond repair, and as he stepped carefully over them his guilt returned and he knew he would have to leave something, to leave some tacit acknowledgement of his part in her circumstances.

With the utmost care, she opened a wooden door hanging by only one hinge, gently leaning the door against the wall so it would make no sound. They were in some sort of courtyard, a small cobbled square littered with junk and rubble and bordered by high stone walls. Still holding his hand in her warm clasp, she wove her way through the debris, helped in part by the newly risen moon, until she brought him to the far wall, away from the house. Here she stopped, backing against a long-abandoned well beneath the tangled branches of an ancient tree, pulling the soldier gently with her.

Still carrying his weapon, the soldier felt the total weight of war settle upon him as he sought a place to rest his rifle. War: the last frontier of human dignity beyond which we are all reduced to the bestial. War: the true human condition in which our base natures are given free rein at the expense of the weak and submissive. War: survival of the strongest as the winner takes all. Despite his desire, the soldier saw the iniquity of his position. But something overrode his sensitivity, allowed his wretched craving to attain ascendancy, and he knew he would do what he had come to do.

And even as he admitted his true instincts to himself, the girl seemed to be his equal in desire. She lifted her arms above her, taking the flimsy rags of her dress over her head, to stand naked in the darkness before him, the gleam of her white skin palely shining within his reach.

'I… There's…'

He wanted to say, *I'm sorry. There's more than this. I want you but I want you decently, without hatred or triumph or malice or…*

'The war,' he whispered hoarsely. 'It's the war,'

The girl seemed not to hear or, if she heard, seemed not to listen. She placed a fingertip to his mouth while her other hand fumbled at his belt in the darkness.

The soldier's hands trembled on her shoulders, shaking as they had during the bombardment while they slid along her arms and back to her neck. She moved a little closer now, the belt undone, the soldier's trousers slipping from his waist. His entire body ached for her as she reached up to his face to plant the lightest of kisses onto his lips.

'If only the war…' he began.

But her mouth closed in on his to still his words, though for the merest fraction of a second.

Gently, she held his face in both her hands as she drew back a little, looking into his eyes. 'Not your war,' she said, as the blades flashed behind him in the moonlight, 'but our war. The old war.'

In less than a heartbeat, before the soldier could lick the taste of her lips from his own, his head was pulled back by the hair and his throat opened to the vertebrae of his neck, a second pair of hands reaching between his legs to strip him, post-mortem, of his power. Almost in the same movement, the three naked women lifted the ruined corpse over the edge of the well, listening to the distant sound of its descent.

Endgame #1

You saw yourself in shades of white
like some invert Joan of Arc
who would burn the citadels
of history in the fires
of enlightenment.

You saw yourself in shades of red
Like the flames consuming
Joan of Arc on Rouen's pyre
before heroic crowds
of barbarians.

You saw yourself in shades of black,
weighted by knowledge,
unknown and unknowable,
that everything gone before
will maybe come again.

You thought you loved all shades of green.
You hated green
And green hated you.

And Who Shall Fight the Peace?

They blew the legs off children and old men
and slaughtered babied mothers
where they ran
for fun and kindness…
until the moment when
the light was blotted out by smoke
and it began
to sound like war in this unwarred city.
Others died from blood loss and weak heart.
Their rattled breaths fading as
the day beyond
was not so much fading
as being torn apart
by the gaping
suppuration of the wound
undressed, festering in fear and putrefied by pity.

We knelt in supplication to an ending
unlikely in our lifetime.
We cried breast-beaten salted tears
impotent against
the rending
of lives cut short
by six-inch spears
and depthless hatred.

We knelt in disbelief where blood pooled
coagulate in spring-warmed
streets, coffee-scented
before the stinking iron stain
clawed into our nostrils, unruled
by humanity,
sanity
sacrificed in two hard flashes as, expectant, we waited.

Then the men came, indignant and unsheathed
with talk of holy vengeance.
And whatever ground was gained
was lost again
in a split-second moment
of sacred indignation.
Their barbed curare words rained
hard onto hearts already double bruised –
once by violence unsought
and once by grief
unbound –
and their words rang false
with venom and unthought
consequence -
mere sound
that landed meaningless amongst the damaged and confused.

They blew the legs off children and soft girls
and so doing rewrote death's rules
on urban vellum
bound in hand-tooled hate.
They changed the ordered logic of the sentient world
to a course of harsh reaction
lest thinking numb
our clamoured warlike vengeance
and its eye-for-eye demands for equal pain.
Or…or are we – the legless, the old, the unbabied –
are we the planters of the bombs
that take away the innocence and blacken the sky
until death falls everywhere as rain
to soak us all?

Can only one side protect us from
the interminable unrelenting sentence?

The Cliché: How It Starts, How It Ends

Evening shadows soak into the wall.
Old feelings
fade and fade
from floor to ceiling
until there's nothing left at all
but stale shade.

When we met I, the nightingale, calling to the sky
With blood rent songs and easy flight, was neon-plumed,
and you, the clown – painted teardrop eye
above smiling downturned mouth – played buffoon,
but softly, holding my feathered breast in your palm.
You cocked your head.
And I was taken like the future shadows by your charm
and we went to bed.

Was it good for me? I wonder now and then, though hindsight
says there's no distinction between that time and all the others
except I think we listened to some music later in that night
when maybe we were tired or hungry or just alone with one another.

We kind of loved I suppose. Briefly, brutally, no quarter given
and no quarter asked as we took what we thought we needed –
salt or salvation or something second minded, driven
by unthought thought. We took the blood and freed it
from its standard iron-stinking race through sclerotic course
to let it spurt
in parabolic arcing for an instant of truthful force.

It's no more than dirt,
this so-called love that sparks, and fires and burns intense for – what?
a breath, passion gasped without tomorrow's eye focused on the where
and on the how and on the reality of our love (and death)? It's a life but not
a love.

Gone are the shadows and gone the wall.
No feelings
to be salvaged
or used in support
of lofty ideals.
It's all shade. All stale.

Just Another Cynical War Story

white lightning flash in a hot spinning night-time of the first kiss as it lands shipwreck-beached on the deserted shores of evening a soft aggressive contact in the dusk

*

a shared hard-to-let flat in the concrete third world of some storm-tossed inner-city…wooden blinkers on the see-no-evil gaze of boarded-up windows where glass has never been…black mould and grey mould and green mould and a smell of damp carpets and long dead cigarettes…

*

he came into the 40-watt room with the cheap taste of low pubs in his mouth and found you talking with the others

you were introduced and – winded by your body-blow beauty – he forgot your name before the sound of it had drowned in the dampness of the walls

he swore at himself for being drunk – for being beyond the circling reach of your conversation

through his stupor's pulsating black void he watched you shine to the music of the autumn lights and blamed the beer and the brandy for falling in love

the others had gone to bed before he realised you were staying overnight and he made an ugly effort to sober up – his frog-bulge stare trying to fix full focal length on anything that couldn't move

his unhooked fish tongue died flapping at the baked dirt-edge pool of his mouth as he tried to speak – to say something that might make you talk to him

his world spun ever faster to the tune of your laughter until the speed reached its limit when his slurring fell away and finally you could talk together and laugh and smoke cigarette after cigarette until both packets lay empty and you knew you were on the edge and looking down

and the kiss landed with the determined stealth of the sea

and your tongues exchanged their secrets

and his hands were in your hair

and your arms around his neck might never let him go

and fragments burst in star-showered brilliance to sprinkle your passion with his perfect love

and fragments burst in star-showered brilliance to sprinkle his passion with your perfect love

and you went to bed

alone

the hammer of his guilt beat against your softly fragile youth and he knew you deserved more than his drunken adoring fumbling so he left you to the wasteland of your single bed while he went to his own room sadly feasting on the yeast-warm tang of your virgin lips

*

You take him water in the morning as he lies crucified beneath a fourteen-year hangover.

'More?' you ask as he lowers the glass from his lips.

He nods without speaking. He knows his voice would be the flat cracked baritone of an Orphean love song to the dead. He closes his eyes, wondering if his breath smells nearly as bad as it tastes.

You come back and sit on the desert of his bed while he empties the second glass.

'You're a shit,' you say, your hands moulding castles on the dunes of the duvet beside his knees. You want to say more, to open the floodgates and deluge his suffering with your own. But you're not sure you can control the undercurrent of real emotion you feel welling inside you.

He looks at you from the bottom of a half-litre of whiskey and he knows he's a shit. He wonders if your reasons for thinking it are the same as his and he doubts it.

He feels he has centre-spread eyes and closes them against the possibility. He can remember drinking with your husband long after you had gone to bed…sharing middle-aged dreams of yesterday's future…protesting…confirming…laughter and promises…vast blank chasms …

'Feeling better?' you ask, hoping you sound sarcastic with the I-don't-care of someone else's wife. Your hands lie still now, truth-naked except for the ring which you wish you had taken off. They rest on the warm quilt and you think how this is the substance of fourteen years: the thickness of a duvet, the lifetime of forever…

You take the glass from his trembling hands and put it on the floor beside the bed as he looks at you more closely than you want, seeing the same girl of his oh-so-long-ago kiss. Only much more beautiful now.

You want to look away but for a long moment you stare into his eyes without expression. Your own eyes are burnished dark and lust-bright with loathing. He takes one of your hands in his and you are surprised at how tightly you hold him. He strokes your fingers and brings them to his lips…

You say, 'Don't,' but the sound has no strength and you pull back your hand only when he takes one of your fingers into his mouth.

'Please,' you say, lowering your eyes to where your hard-locked grasp writhes in your lap. You feel your own heat radiating through your jeans and behind his shield of whiskey fumes you sense the same heat rising in him. Eighteen inches… fourteen years…two lifetimes…The distance between you stretches like razor wire until you think it might snap, until you know it must snap and …

He falls back against the pillow and the spell is broken. 'I love you,' he says. 'I always have and you know it.'

His voice is as quiet and dead as the breeze in a photograph and you know what he says is the truth and you wonder if he said it or if you said it but you don't care whether or not he loves you because of the fourteen years.

'Shut up,' you whisper in a red twist of uncertainty, daring yourself but holding back.

He touches your perfect cheek with the scraps of his fingertips and you lift your eyes to him once more. You say nothing but he listens to the dark suns of your eyes as they set below the horizon of their tears and he knows you are fighting the silence and fighting what lies behind that silence with your lip-lost mouth gouging a deep scratch on polished steel. When he touches your ear you flinch, hoping he won't draw your face to his…hoping he won't…wanting him to… And you despise him for your weakness.

'If you come to bed, we can talk about it,' he says.

But you can't see his smile because your eyes are closed. There is a screaming in your ears which you hope is only on the inside and you are shaking your head more violently than you want but you can't stop.

'Hey,' he says softly, the sigh of skin-brushed silk. 'Hey, I'm joking. Come on.'

He raises your head with a finger under your chin and you grab his hand and kiss the backs of his fingers with a greed which denies his words and almost makes him speak the one-way street of his heart.

But you speak instead. From somewhere near to drowning, you break the surface and emerge into the light of safety in triumph over your own desire and his desire and…and your husband's desire, if only you knew it.

'Leave me alone,' you say. And you look him in the eyes again and your tears have gone, dried by the heat of your sudden anger. 'You don't know how bloody dangerous you are.'

He reads the pity and contempt on your face and he knows you think he is playing with you. Only your still holding his hand so tightly prevents him from using harsh words.

'Love is dangerous,' he says, 'not me.' And his voice is sad in the knowledge that your misplaced morality is ultimately unshakeable. 'Love is dangerous because it makes us behave the way we really are. We lose control and we can't always cope with that. So we deny love. I love you very much.'

'Don't, please.' Black and white, hysteria's disc-flat circles spin towards vertigo in the hollowness of your stomach. You still have his hand in yours but you want your nails in his flesh, your teeth in his flesh; you want the taste of his blood on your tongue.

'I don't believe you,' you say, even though you do believe him, because he is speaking for you as well as for himself. 'I don't believe you because you love whoever you're with at the time. You lie in your love and I could never trust you.'

Your words thrust holes through the morning's flimsy skin and he feels the many shades of his pain seeping out into the no-hiding-place of the day.

He knows that what you say is no more than inspired self-protection but he also knows his mistake is old and immovable, crusted over by the coral of conversations which never took place.

*

sunday lunchtime the day after you'd met – six hours after he had tasted the moon on your breath and bathed your vulnerability in the tears of his loss

you sit in the dim quiet of a public bar with three or four friends and irrelevant drinks on the table

he sees only you and tries not to make a fool of himself

he was hungover then too and he lit a cigarette to calm his rattling hands but he was sucking the sodden fur of a ginger cat and he crushed it out in the ashtray two seats away you were cool and distant and avoided looking in his direction

he thought this was a denial and let the accumulation of his whole life conspire against the single silver truth of himself – let all the falseness of convention overwhelm and subdue that one thing that was his desire

instead he watched you leave the pub to drive back to the coast and your safe life and he drank the bitter grief of his beer through the chewed unspoken words of his yearning

you left he watched

his mistake was made in doing nothing

he found your phone number in his flatmate's address book but couldn't bring himself to dial it for all the bastard reasons of doubt and insecurity conjured by your averted gaze

shortly afterwards life changed

he moved away to the north although he thought of you in the darkness of his nights as you remembered him for a while like the smile of a stranger in a dream

and the next time you met you were a married woman

*

Your argument works only because your ears are stopped against him.

'It only holds true from your position.' He knows you won't listen but he owes it to himself so he says it anyway. 'I'm bound to seem to love whoever I'm with at the time because when you see that, I'm with you. So it's true. When you're not there, you can't see that I don't love whoever is.'

His voice has risen a little and you glance towards the door. You can hear your husband moving about downstairs in the kitchen and you wonder just what you are doing sitting on this bed holding the hand of your never-lover while the man you are married to (and who you love who you love) makes tea and noise against the background sounds of your voices. If only it could…

'Also,' relentless word-mill of lies, of truth, of you don't know what. 'I never realised… You never –'

'Did I need to?' You spit the words with a cracked glass frown on your perfect brow as if the question was born in a film you've never seen.

He doesn't answer and his silence makes it difficult to think.

'If only the world would stop for three weeks,' you say, hot salt blinding your eyes. 'If only we could have three weeks together.'

'Three weeks?' He laughs – but gently because he has just now understood that you don't understand. 'I'm not talking about a fling,' he says with patience, his words smoothing the creases on the crumpled bedsheet of your thinking. His fingers tighten around your grateful hand. 'I love you enough for the world to stop for three centuries.'

Without listening, you hear the sounds of his words. You are already three weeks away. You absently reach out to pluck a tiny hair from his chest as you think how you would feel for those three weeks. Only his sudden stillness brings you back to what you have just done and you lean towards him to kiss the invisible wound with a magic potency that explodes at the base of his skull. Your lips linger for an instant to prolong this, the third kiss, as you consider…

You turn your slow-motion head and rest your cheek against his chest and slide your hand over the whiskey-reeking surface of his skin in a caress which is the closest you can come to surrender.

You know the emotion between you is undeniable and destructive. It must be nailed to resolve's unyielding board with rods of fortitude… But not yet. You stroke his chest and circle his nipple with abandoned fingertips safe in the knowledge that your time will soon run out.

His hand is on your face, moving over your face like the blush of guilt which is already there. And he nuzzles in the fragrance of your hair, dreaming you and wanting you and crying inside for the lost moments past and the lost moments to come, feeling your cruel touch on him and knowing that you could never see that cruelty because you think he is too hard to hurt and too insensitive to care.

You lie against him for twelve minutes as the red second hand of the alarm clock winds through the morning while he tries to insinuate himself deeper into your thoughts, telling you that it's all true, that whether you like it or not, neither of you can ever escape.

When you sit up, there's a redness around your eyes which will fade before lunch. 'You'd better get up,' you say. 'You've made a ruin of my life.'

As you stand, you lean over him once more and touch his forehead with your lips in a kiss as soft as the shadow of a moth's wing before you leave the bedroom without looking back.

aside

I look at my life and I think 'this is
a life lived in parentheses.'

You Leave Tomorrow

You leave tomorrow. All your luggage
packed and labelled
like museum pieces sent to storage,
lost to years in cold rooms –
bedclothes, kitchenware, shirts and shoes
all neatly ordered and forgotten
(not the stuff of posterity or interest really)
until you reach your destination when you choose
which boxes should be left unopened.

… Tonight the sky
is flat and green:
an undercoat on which the dye
of ageing slowly leaks.
And then white hot stars
and then the starash cold of
early dawn
and then tomorrow
and you'll be gone.

You leave tomorrow as you always will.
A Pickford life.
Each unfulfilled moment
a locked cage, a shooting star,
an abandoned box
in the non-museum.
Unlock the cage
and follow the shooting star
and open the forgotten box.

Tonight the city air is thick with swifts
carving scimitar and black.
They'll be gone before the summer's over
but come next year, they'll be back.

Analysis

The silence between two thoughts
is where quick life teems.
Infinite possibilities synapsed
separately
like bookends
that bracket the world's great events
shut tight against discovery.

Silence smothered by extremes –
tea and Kant perhaps
(you), raincoats, seeds and other nonsense (me) –
one voice that sends
words unsent
to a place beyond recovery
where, tired, we've already fought.

It's personal.
I hate your bloodied elbows and bad breath.
I hate the way you walk and I hate your filthy nails.
I hate your submissive slide towards inevitable death.
And I hate you in my bed with all that that entails
(as though I'm supernumerary to your last gasp desperate fight
to prove some final triumph over the darkness of another night).
I hate your unsmart clothes and scratching cheek.
I hate the rancid hairs uncurling from your nose.
I hate the way you look and I hate the way you speak
and I really hate my nakedness when your desperation grows
as though I'm supernumerary to your last gasp flailing flight
to prove your final triumph in our never-ending fight.

It's personal.
You hate my trivial thinking and cheap clothes.
You hate the way I drive and you hate the things I eat.
You hate the music that I listen to and the way my hard breath blows
when I struggle in the sickness of defeat
(as though you're not supernumerary to my dying or my living,
to the redemptive force of healing through easily forgiving).
You hate my inner woman and my assertion.
You hate my heavy heart and my far too frequent weeping.
You hate my lack of interest in naked hard exertion
and you really hate my wakefulness as you drift off into sleeping
because you know you're supernumerary to my solitary survival
in the redemptive state of healing where in strength I stand unrivalled.

The silence between two thoughts…
refuge from the fight…
breathing space…bent double…hands held hard
on hips…downcast
eyes and heart…
knowing now the fight, lost at last,
was always lost. Time has passed.

A la Recherche du Guerres Perdues

1

2003, 20 March. US and UK forces invaded Iraq on the pretext of protecting the Iraqi people from its own leader, the 'dictator' or 'war criminal', Saddam Hussein, in the first strike of what has become known as the Second Gulf War. As almost the first initiative in this manufactured war, Iraq's oil fields and refineries were seized. Later, when the coalition forces entered Baghdad, a protective cordon of coalition troops was erected around the building of the Oil Ministry while the rest of the city – the rest of the government buildings – were left unattended, unguarded targets for arsonists and looters. So, why protect only the Oil Ministry building?

The simple answer goes to the very heart of the cause of the war itself: the Oil Ministry was known to house thousands of seismic maps, priceless keys to the untapped treasures of future exploration across the country. These were more than the trophies, more than the spoils that went to the victors: these maps and the treasure they pinpointed were the veritable *raison d'être* for the offensive in the first place. Oil.

But there was oil – vast amounts of oil – throughout most of the countries of the Middle East. What was the lure of Iraqi oil in particular? Why was this specific country invaded – again – for its sole global resource? What made Iraqi oil so special? Indeed, was it special? If history is examined closely, it can be seen that during the ninety or so years leading up to the 2003 invasion there have been eight distinct wars on Iraqi soil and all of them have been waged in the name of oil. Iraqi oil is a high-grade product which is cheap to produce and abundant. These three factors – quality, price and supply – offer enormous profit to any company able to access possibly the world's most valuable commodity and, if the companies involved are linked to the governments of their home countries, the vast profits can be shared at administrative level through taxation, follow-on wealth generation via GDP and export currency from selling on petrochemical products. Oil is money and Iraq has deposits of it in spades. At the time of the 2003 invasion, the country's reserves were estimated at 112 billion barrels, an estimate which ranks it second only to Saudi Arabia in revenue potential. The US Department of Energy, however, believed this figure was too low, believed that the real reserves of oil in Iraq might be as much as 400 billion barrels, an estimate echoed in an interview granted to Platts, an industry information bulletin, on 22 May 2002. Iraq's senior deputy oil minister claimed that his country's production would exceed 300 billion barrels 'when all Iraq's regions are explored'. Not only would Iraq become the number one producer in the world (surpassing Saudi Arabia) but the relative cheapness in extracting the oil from the ground could see company profits reach $US5 trillion. Five million million dollars.

The attraction of Iraqi oil becomes self-evident.

ii

2003. Annual revenue figures for ExxonMobil, the world's largest oil company, stood at $US247 billion, more than the revenues of 185 of the world's countries, including Holland, Sweden, Brazil and Canada. In fact, only the revenues of the US, UK, France, Germany, Italy and Japan were higher than those of ExxonMobil at that time. Its recorded profits for 2003 stood at $US22 billion, more than the combined profits of Ford, General Motors, Chrysler and Toyota. Oil is bigger than big business. And the protection of oil assets is bigger still.

iii

At the beginning of the twentieth century, the smut-filled world of coal and steam was suddenly in the throes of a new fuel revolution. The potential of oil was being recognised, as with many commodities, many scientific developments, by the military: hitherto cumbersome ships reliant on stokers shovelling vast mounds of coal into furnaces day and night were being replaced in Britain by the Dreadnought class of destroyer, a vessel powered by the cleaner, more ergonomic and more storage-efficient fuel – oil. Even before 1910, British warships could travel further, faster, with fewer port calls for refuelling: once again, Britannia ruled the waves.

Nor was it only the navy who benefited from the new fuel. The First World War saw the first use of the motor car as a military vehicle, the first use of truck transport for men and munitions and all manner of supplies, the first use of motorised tanks at the Battle of the Somme, the first use of aeroplanes as a military option. And all these modes of transportation, even more so then than now, were 'gas-guzzlers' in constant need of replenishment. Both sides in the war ate up oil at a phenomenal rate and both sides faced severe shortages until the allies eventually prevailed through greater supplies. As Lord Curzon remarked in parliament at the end of the 1914–1918 war, 'the Allied cause has floated to victory upon a wave of oil'.

But the fuel had to come from somewhere and companies at the forefront of technology and commercial *savoir faire* were prospecting, exploring, drilling and refining. And selling their product to traditionally the world's biggest consumer: the military. By 1911, Royal Dutch Shell and Standard Oil were global companies with interests in Indonesia, Russia, Romania, North America, Mexico and South America. And these interests were served by fleets of railcars, tankers, storage facilities. Standard Oil's fleet of oil tankers numbered almost one hundred. In 1911, oil was already serious business. It is no accident today that financial reports include oil prices alongside currency cross-rates as the benchmark of the nation's economy. And during the First World War a significant amount of both Allied and German oil came from the region now called Iraq.

In fact, it could be argued that the first of the eight oil wars to be fought in Iraq was the war of colonial conquest, 1914–1918. Britain fabricated a flimsy tissue of excuses to infiltrate an established area of the Ottoman Empire, an empire in which German engineers were constructing an extensive rail system that would help transport oil directly from the region to, possibly, the German military machine. Britain prevailed and the Turks – and their railway – were eventually defeated, pushed out of the areas of Baghdad, Kirkuk and Mosul, the areas which controlled the flow of oil in the region. History has shown that oil was the major factor in shaping British foreign policy at that time, with Sir Maurice Hankey claiming in a government cabinet letter that oil was a 'first class war aim'. And, to prove that this was the case, London ordered its armies to continue the war after the armistice had been signed until Mosul had been taken. This was in direct contravention of the secret Sykes-Picot agreement of 1915, which had promised precisely this region to the French as payment for their support in the campaign.

Having effectively stolen Mosul and, therefore, Mosul's resources, Britain then embarked on the second Iraqi oil war, the War of Pacification, 1918–1930, to protect its new assets. Crushing an insurrection in 1920, Britain continued to suppress insurgents, using poison gas, bombs, aeroplane attacks and an army of occupation largely drawn from the Indian Army. Villages were burned, taxes exacted and Iraqis killed as Britain sought to consolidate its holdings in the oil fields from Basra to Baghdad and beyond. Even after granting nominal independence to the country in 1932, Britain maintained an occupation force in the country, continuing to rule albeit indirectly, through a strong influence over the imported Royal family of King Faisal, his son Ghazi, and his son Faisal II.

This influence, however, was not enough to persuade Britain that Iraq was safe from the Axis early in the Second World War and in 1941 the country was once again reoccupied by British forces. And, again, the driving motivation for the occupation was protection of the oil fields – as much this time, though, from the US as from the Germans: just because the US were allies didn't mean that Britain had to share her sweeties with them if she could avoid it.

The fourth Iraq oil war didn't occur until 1980, when Iraq attacked Iran in a savage eight-year conflict that resulted in many hundreds of thousands of casualties on both sides, and the destruction of vast areas of both countries' oil fields and supply infrastructure. Behind this particularly bloody war lurked foreign governments who harboured vested interests, not so much in the outcome, as in the process, foreign governments who fostered the conflict for their own ends. The US and the UK supplied arms to Iraq, supplied military training and the ability to produce chemical and biological weaponry. France and Russia and Germany also became involved with armaments provision to prolong the war: the longer the war lasted, the longer Iraqi and Iranian oil supplies were suspended to the rest of the world and the higher oil prices soared to bring even bigger profits to the major oil companies. As James Paul claimed in his paper to the UN Global Policy Forum in November 2003, 'By bankrupting the two governments and ruining their oil infrastructure, the war also potentially opened the way for the return of the [oil] companies through privatisation in the not-too-distant future.'

The superpowers, however, were to be thwarted: after the war ended in 1988, Iraq and Iran turned to Japanese oil companies in their quest for investment – including a Japanese role in Iraq's monumental Majnoun oil field. Europe and the Unites States were panicked: they could not allow control of the world's greatest modern resources to fall into the hands of the Japanese. Something would have to be done to prevent such an unthinkable event.

That something was the First Gulf War: the fifth oil war.

Endgame #2

We turned off the light and nothing changed;
no softened romance
or breathy song,
no sweet-scented smoke
to float us giggling into the night.
Just hard wattage,
a final fucking on the unmade bed
to Piaf or Como or
some other scratchy crooner
in the room. The smoke
was acrid, harsh and laughter-free.
I slept while you stumbled
off into the street.

A Hundred Years From Now In Both Directions

There were trenches
in the rain
where mud and death
lay deep,
obliterating all senses,
where screaming pain,
that with each breath,
increased.

One hundred years
the same
but for the change of forces
in the line
where the vanquished wears
the name
that usually endorses
the benign.

To the victor, what?
The spoils?
Me and all I am
is all
until my self, not now forgot,
recoils
from that bloodless sham,
enthralled.

There are trenches
in the rain
where vermin crawled and ran
and hid
while the gas bomb quenches
that screaming pain
that might kill a lesser man –
and did.

One hundred years
the same
(save for the effect and cause,
which change)
though the battle song appears
to sing your name
now, whereas all those times before
silence reigned.

*

You, the flea,
you carry in your eternal bite,
the pathogen of love,
harbinger of hate,
presager of the end.

I, the disease,
incubated in the long night,
watch you from above
and patiently await
the chance to become your friend.

*

A future misted vague
in shrouded possibility
that denies the fucking plague
its gross inevitability.

Gallipoli 2015 #2

The last witness dead.
Only the crusted remnants
of other slaughters – Tobruk,
Long Tan, Derapet – look on,
mouths chicken-arsed in vinegar disapproval,
chests festooned in baubled glory.
Some tears. Some self-righteous triumph
at having made it through another pointless year.

In Martin Place a pre-dawn crowd
huddles in mawkish tribute before the long march
down George Street with the maimed
and damaged and all-year-long ignored.
A few hours of two-up in the pub, cheap beers
and a fading to insignificance until next year.

A War That's Not A War

Pink shit
Pink…shit
Pink…... shit
Pink…… .… shit
Pink………… .… shit
Pink………..……shit
Pink……………... shit
Pink…………………shit
Pink……………………. shit
Pink………………………..shit
Pink……………………….… shit
Pink……………………………..shit
Pink……………………………… shit
Pink…………………………………..shit
Pink……………………………………. shit
Pink………………………………………..shit
Pink………………………………………… shit
Pink……………………………………………..shit
Pink…………………………………………………. shit
Pink……………………………………………………..shit
Pink……………………………………………………… shit
Pink………………………………………………………….shit
Pink
Shit

Kite

Go. Bring the wind
and fly me like a kite.
Send me thermal-riding
      skyward –
      arcing against restraint –
            against the pull of anchored cord –
towards unbounded chaos – freedom –
                  liberty…
Now ease a little and unwind
slack string to see a slight
pause before the twisting, diving
      earthward
      double-barrelled feint –
      submissive, defeated, bored –
      before resurgent upthrust for one
              last try…

The kite, catenaried between then
and now
              between
      land and sky
dances like some wing-clipped captive
bird above.

Stop. Quench the wind. Reel me in.
I've had enough.

A la Recherché du Guerres Perdues (Part 2)

The Iraqi invasion of Kuwait in August 1990 saw the annexation of Kuwaiti oil fields by Saddam Hussein, a move that the conventional perspective on history believes shook the foundations of Western superpower thinking. In fact, the Kuwait invasion was almost certainly orchestrated by the US–UK alliance. The response was swift: US military force was deployed to the area with the backing of the UK and France. After all, there was an enormous amount at stake: as George Bush Senior explained, 'Our jobs, our way of life, our own freedom and the freedom of friendly countries around the world would all suffer if control of the world's great oil reserves fell into the hands of Saddam Hussein.' Of course, there was no threat to 'our jobs' or the 'freedom of friendly countries' if those very oil reserves were held in the hands of a few foreign companies far distant from the land in which the oil lay. Especially if some of those companies were directly controlled by the Bush family...

Iraq was bombed. Many of its cities and military installations were destroyed, before a ground offensive was launched to retake Kuwait, an offensive which also threatened to overthrow the Iraqi government. The US-led troops, for whatever reason – possibly because the US had effectively installed Hussein in power in the first place – stopped short of marching into Baghdad and toppling Hussein, seemingly satisfied to have regained control over the flow of oil and having severely battered the country. Up to 100,000 casualties were recorded in the few short months of fighting.

The troops didn't leave the country once order had been reestablished, however. Despite the parlous state of Iraq as a whole, the US–UK coalition could not afford to let slip the reins by which they controlled the oil: they had to remain in the country, again as an army of occupation, to safeguard their investment. And, again, the local population resented the foreign intruders, rising against them in a resistance movement of insurgency, thereby instigating the sixth Iraqi oil war, a low intensity war of attrition between 1991 and 2003. The Western allies reacted on all fronts. Using military force, they quashed, as far as possible, all resistance to the occupation while bringing to bear huge economic pressure through UN sanctions – which they prevented the Security Council from lifting by using their power of veto. Iraq's economy was strangled, its oil sales were restricted and the country's oil industry disrupted to the point of near-non-operation. Once more, with the global flow of oil stemmed as Iraqi oil was effectively off the market, the huge profits of the major oil companies grew even more huge as prices climbed steadily. Meanwhile, the ordinary people of the occupied country continued to suffer.

During this period, a number of attempts were made on Saddam Hussein's life, attempts instigated, if not actually carried out, by the US–UK coalition. It remains debatable as to whether these attempts were serious in their intent, or whether they were merely window-dressing to suggest that Hussein would not be tolerated while, in reality, he was being allowed to continue to function in a controlled manner. The occupation forces also launched major air strikes against Iraqi military targets, notably in January 1993, January 1996, June 1996 and December 1998. It has been argued many times that, had the coalition genuinely wanted to oust Saddam Hussein, had the US and UK, with the support of other European governments, genuinely wanted to overthrow the Iraqi government during this time, it would have been a relatively easy task. So what prevented them from carrying out their stated objective? UN sensibility? Hardly, given that the two countries had already vetoed UN anti-sanctions motions: consideration of the United Nations Security Council would have reasonably extended no further than a stated intent followed by a swift execution followed by short-lived condemnation. Then, if not to placate the UN, why did the Western forces hold back? There are three real reasons for going no further than the previously mentioned window-dressing: the first was the fear of an Arab backlash. Saudi Arabia still retained the pole position of global oil producer and, despite the Saudis' strong relationships with the US, any overly anti-Arab move would excite the whole region on a racial basis that Saudi Arabia could not politically ignore. Oil supplies would almost certainly have to be suspended altogether. Secondly, the Islamic threat would be further activated if an essentially unprovoked coup took place. Muslims from around the world would take arms against the 'Christian' invaders, hitting soft targets with terrorist attacks which would leave the aggressors vulnerable to ostracism amongst their own. (This, of course, has subsequently happened leaving the world in a destabilised and terrorist-threatened state, although whose hand is at the helm remains a contentious question.)

And thirdly, during the 1990s a number of oil companies from other parts of the world were trying to negotiate deals with the Iraqi government: by prolonging the conflict situation, the coalition put on a show of force that discouraged any attempted infiltration of the market. Production could easily be interrupted by air strikes against foreign installations mistakenly thought to be under Iraqi control. And while Saddam Hussein remained in power there was always the possibility of further military action in the country. It was unlikely that foreign investment would be poured into so volatile a market.

However, by 2003 there had been enough propagandist manoeuvring, enough insinuation of deviousness to persuade the world (or those parts of it that wielded the various powers to condemn or condone) that Iraq was concealing weapons of mass destruction and that the only solution – for the survival of the entire planet – was the immediate removal of Saddam Hussein. Once again, despite almost universal opposition, the US–UK coalition launched the seventh Iraqi oil war.

We now know that there were no weapons of mass destruction; there was no 'smoking gun'. But such was the state of hysteria by 20 March 2003, hysteria induced by Western press scare stories fed to the news agencies by Western government spokesmen, that the American and European public on the whole supported their troops' invasion of Saddam's 'mad dog' regime. Saddam was removed, his government overthrown. The US and UK took over direct rule of the country and, by default (?), the country's oil fields. Again. And again, the Iraqi people were the ones who suffered as their economy was destroyed, their lands were destroyed, their government was destroyed. But as we know, the spirit of the Iraqi people was not destroyed. Armed resistance has continued and still continued in 2008 as the eighth Iraqi oil war took place. Another war of pacification. Another war that the coalition could not win because history has shown us that suppression inevitably ends in the repulsion of the invader. It might take generations but the outcome should never be in doubt: the US-led forces of occupation in Iraq (under whatever spurious flag – whether it be the flag of peace, the flag of protection, the flag of democracy) will be repulsed simply because they should not be there in the first place. Oil or no oil, Iraq belongs to its people, Iraq belongs to…Iraqis.

Endgame #3

'I think it's time that you two…'
I said that.
I saw how you lay at the end of thirteen years,
wrapped around each other…naked…
What should I think?
What I should think is that the time had come,
that you should wake up and…

Thirteen years…a bet:
'I can get her into bed
In two days…'
And you said, 'two hours'
and won the prize.

You won the prize
while I… I lost the game
that my life
turned into
as you played each card to trump my own:
your winning tricks
a theft…
you stole my argument
        and my choice
you stole my breath
        and my dream
you stole my endgame
        and you stole my face
you stole my interest
        and my heat
you stole my grasp
        and my justice

you stole my passion
        and my grief
you stole everything
until I, at last,
hated you
and me.
Until, at last,
you lay bitched in bed
and I woke you to
the light of
betrayal.
Who won?

What it means

'It means nothing.' The words
slip past my smiling teeth
like the shadows of timid birds
or the ghost-scent insinuation of the thief.

'Something, nothing: it means
what it means.' Dark and light,
the threshold breached, it seems
you've accepted my specious offer of the night.

The night is long and short, coal-black and gold,
and fanfared in a tinnitus blaring.
Relentless rain in ceaseless pouring drowns
the most secluded garden with pure cold
hatred. The night is hard and brutal, as uncaring
and unyielding as abandoned slagheap mounds.

Western haiku

Seventeen dark years –
a domestic white-noise war.
Sound: a pin dropping.

Bury the Dead

The churchyard was empty save for gravestones and wind. Leached monochrome clay soaked, in dark gradation, the trees and the dogstooth moulding and the lancet windows, frugal in their narrow arching. Leaves, damp and blackened were ripped from skeleton branches of gnarled trees and slapped against the gravel path, occasionally sticking to the dank stones where they tumbled and fell.

Samuel yawed arthritic up the three steps into the porch and steadied his balance one-handed against the damp wall. He took off his cap and ran a long and spotted hand over the few wisps of hair drifting like threadbare smoke across the mottled skin of his scalp. The porch smelled of hymn books and mildew and felt somehow even colder than the bone-cold winter air outside.

With his head age-bowed, he shuffled into the main body of the church and sidled into the empty rear pew to his left. He stuffed his rolled-up cap into his jacket pocket and wiped his hands on the trousers of his one dark suit as he sat down. At his age, funerals made his palms itch and he often wondered if the discomfort was caused by guilt at being one of those left behind by so many who were younger.

Before him, the Early-English-style church was filled in echoing susurration with the scuffling sounds of impatient feet and the murmurous sounds of subdued voices as people settled into place like bedding animals, waiting for the service to begin. An occasional soft cough punctuated the overall soughing as someone cleared a throat or exorcised their nervousness, but all noise ceased when the vicar pushed himself to his feet in a swirl of surplice, a silence spreading like sleep over the congregation. All eyes followed his stately movement towards the carved eagle lectern that glared out over the assembled mourners before being drawn back once again to the altar steps on which the coffin lay.

The eulogy began and as the vicar's words floated up into the stone vaulting above his head, Samuel looked around the church. The small nave was very nearly full. It was a good turnout, he thought. But that was no more than you would expect, for Sarah had lived in the village all her life and had been well liked. Samuel knew all the mourners and nodded his approval at their being there, feeling their loss as his loss and sharing with them a common bereavement. Each in his or her own way had been linked to Sarah – more, he thought, to their advantage than to her own, as she had been one of life's natural givers, asking little in return. Casting his eyes over the individual members of the congregation, he considered the debts to be repaid her when the various times came and, as he did so, he sensed a movement behind him, felt the presence of some latecomer in the change in the air pressure inside the church as the outer door was opened.

Turning stiffly, ratcheting his calcified vertebrae through a few reluctant degrees, he glanced over his shoulder to see Ralph Sawyer slip into the rear pew on the other side of the central aisle to where Samuel was sitting. For a long moment, Samuel sat effigiac in unmoving and expressionless consideration of the late arrival, watching as the other glared about him as though challenging anyone to his right to be there.

Ralph Sawyer's green eyes were as hard as they had ever been as he stared down the aisle to where the coffin rested, and the hard stare drew an impenetrable barrier across his thoughts as though to protect his thinking from discovery or even from scrutiny. Within the village, only Ralph had had little contact with Sarah, only Ralph had nothing good to say about her. Not that he had ever said anything against her: he simply never let her name pass his lips. In his taciturn way, Ralph allowed his feelings to show only through the set of his mouth, the narrowing of his eyes. Fifty years had passed since he and Sarah had spoken to each other, since she had given up trying. Even after they had buried Ruben, when Sarah had become a young widow, Ralph continued to ignore her in the street.

Samuel sighed in remembering as the vicar's ululate voice purled the ancient stones overhead. He'd watched them lower Ruben into the ground and he'd watched as Sarah had grown old alone, one day at a time. And all down the long years Ralph had hardened and had become desiccate and he had never married. And now Ralph's fiery red hair had quietened to a dull rust and Sarah was dead.

He must be well over eighty, now, Samuel thought.

As the vicar's kindness droned into the vaulting, freshly pressed handkerchiefs dabbed at blurred faces and shoulders hunched and shuddered in small acts of grieving.

Samuel could see the head of Sarah's son in the front pew, a bowed and respectful head gone grey these last few years. Young Ruben would be nearing fifty, he supposed, maybe even older. A headstrong youth grown into the most responsible of men, his fierce temper had been subdued by the gentility of his mother and the tolerance of his father until the malice of his peers at the brightness of his hair and his cat's eye gleam dwindled through boredom. His parents had been immensely proud of him when he'd gone into business, quickly becoming successful through hard fair dealing and ability, although they'd worried enough when they learned how much he'd had to borrow from the bank at the beginning. Samuel smiled to himself as he remembered the night the elder Ruben found out. Sitting in the public bar of the Shepherd worrying aloud about his son's financial affairs. He was drunk by the time Young Ruben came in to reassure him and take him home. But all that was in the past now, and Young Ruben wasn't so young any more.

The congregation was kneeling. Samuel leaned incrementally forwards and rested the bones of his arms on the back of the hardwood pew in front: his knees no longer let him lower himself to the hassock so he made do sitting with bowed head over clasped hands. And as he sat in his own unfathomed silence, his line of sight was unbroken by those ahead and he could see the coffin, butter yellow with gleaming brass fittings and looking too small to be the cause of so much sorrow. Above it, the clergyman recited his practised lines, his fingers interlocked beneath his paunch.

Samuel glanced across the aisle and watched Ralph Sawyer scowl down the length of the nave and he wondered what nonsense was in the other man's mind to cause such a fierceness in his expression. Even if there had been reason enough once for Ralph Sawyer to scowl, that reason, surely, was in the past now and, Samuel thought, bitter fools like Ralph Sawyer would do well to bury that past with Sarah today.

The pallbearers bent to the coffin and raised it insubstantial from the altar steps and balanced it on their shoulders as if it weighed nothing. They were the undertaker's men, of course, professional coffin-carriers in sombre suits from the town down the mountain, towards the coast. Professional coffin-carriers…

It used to be the family – husbands, sons and brothers – who carried the dead, who took care of their own in the last ritual of intimacy. But no more. That ritual, too, was a long time ago. Samuel had seen the changes but was unconvinced; on reflection, he wondered if the old traditions weren't the better. It seemed somehow…more right – more conclusive – for those who were closest to be involved to the end. But then again… The sombre-clad bearers passed between the banked mourners and the mourners fell in behind the lengthening procession like some macabre polonaise or like dark waters falling in on the trough trawled behind a slow boat. Sighing and inclining his head as Sarah was carried past the end of his pew, his thoughts again drifted briefly to Ralph Sawyer and his inconclusive involvement in Sarah's life…

As he had been almost the last to enter the church, so he was the last to leave, following the other mourners into the bleak morning air of the churchyard. Against the heavy white sky, rooks swirled like shreds of charred paper above the black-etched branches of the winter trees. All black, Samuel thought: birds and trees and the people below.

He took his cap from his pocket and held it tightly, still rolled, in knotted hands, the wind lifting his wispy hair like fine white threads. He stood a little apart from the others without really knowing why, and he saw, beyond the vicar, that Ralph Sawyer also stood apart, huddled inside his old black suit with the lapels of his jacket pulled together against the bitter swirling of the wind.

Once more, the clergyman intoned the service but his words were snatched away by the gusts that slapped coats and skirts against blue-cold legs and that grabbed at the grimly held hats on the women's heads. The clergyman held onto the book with both hands lest the pages be ripped out and scattered among the wet grass and haphazard headstones like some sort of confetti for the dead.

Samuel shivered and the wind stung his face and the stinging brought a kind of focus to his thinking and he suddenly saw the many small ways in which he would miss Sarah. He would miss their few brief words as she passed his cottage on her way to the post office on a Thursday morning and he would miss the shared moments as he made his way up here to the churchyard on a summer's Sunday afternoon if she happened to be pottering in her garden when he went by. Like everyone else in the village, he supposed, he would miss her in simply knowing that she was no longer there.

They were lowering the box into the hole now and tears were standing out like glass tracery on Young Ruben's cheeks. Yes, Samuel thought, those left behind are the ones who hurt the most. He looked past the vicar to Ralph Sawyer, still glowering at the coffin after it had sunk from view so that he glowered unseeing at the space where it had been. Suddenly he seemed to rouse himself, raising his face so that the eyes of the two old men met across the cold earth, and Samuel wondered again at the strength of such emotion. Surely it was impossible that this could be the accumulated venom of fifty years' denial? Of fifty years' knowledge of having once been cheated…? That that hatred had burned fiercely at first was true enough, when Sarah had chosen Ruben over Ralph despite everything. But it must have subsided long ago, must have diminished to become a smouldering grudge and then no more than a habit thence to disappear altogether, even in so obstinate and peevish a man as

Ralph Sawyer. The old fool would hardly venture out on a day like this for a brief moment of spiteful triumph – the triumph of having outlived the woman who had refused him a half century earlier? Yet the expression on his face was unmistakable. And as Samuel watched, Young Ruben lifted his gaze to that of Ralph Sawyer and for a split second there was something there, something alive and quick in the twinned green burning of their eyes, but something which was gone as quickly as it came.

Samuel sadly shook his head and turned aside as the first handfuls of earth spattered onto the wooden coffin in a muted chamade. Slowly, people began to move away then, to walk along the gravel path talking in quiet voices, glad it was all over, pleased to have come. Beside the grave the son stood a while longer, his wife waiting at the lychgate, and then he, too, moved away with slow grief towards his mother's cottage for tea and consolation and time for remembrance.

Samuel looked around to find Ralph Sawyer gone. He was alone in the churchyard and he stepped onto the gravel path and fitted his cap onto his head. Yes, he thought again, he would miss Sarah. And as he shut the gate behind him, he stood peacefully on the pavement and thought that perhaps he understood Ralph Sawyer's feelings after all. Perhaps the hatred had remained there for all those years, unseen, being directed inwards. Perhaps it was the self-hatred of a man who, by his own stubbornness, had already missed Sarah for half a century, and who had never grieved his loss until today. But today had proved too long in coming so that his grief was a withered thing wasted beneath the cancerous rot of self-pity, unable to surface, to free itself and find expression.

Thrusting his hands deep into his pockets, Samuel hoped

that he was wrong, hoped that another explanation better fitted what he had seen and what he knew, and he set out for his own cottage, where the fire would still be burning in the living room and the kettle was ready on the hob where he had left it.

Blindsided: A Song of Innocence and Experience

i

Do you get much time for reading these days, Auntie Jane?
Can you focus on the pages? Do you understand the words?
Or have you dropped the unread book to lie rotting in the rain
while smiling death and crying life portrayed between the covers shows
how you and life and death are unquestionably absurd?

Do you get much time for talking these days, Auntie Jane?
Can you focus on the thesis? Do you understand the thought?
Or have all your words unspoken blocked the synapses of your brain
to runnel burning tears of silence down ancient papery cheeks while all
around you no-one notices how mutely you're distraught?

Do you get much time for laughing these days, Auntie Jane?
Can you focus on the story? Do you understand the joke?
Or has the humour all deserted you as you suffer from the strain
of simply trying to remember in whose comedy you once starred
when the final curtain falls with all your unspoken lines revoked?

Do you get much time for fucking these days, Auntie Jane?
Can you focus on the pleasure? Do you understand the need?
Or are your breasts untouched and limp, your pleasure unentertained
by lovers' lengthy measure, and has the venal urge abandoned you since
your long-ago female being was beached by the tidal bleed?

ii

questions asked
like salt grains
scattered on
the table…
ignored
or
hardly worth
acknowledgement…
barely worth
an answer.
Or, if an answer like some crumb-brush
is required,
then let it leave the table clean.
Unsalted.
A pristine surface
unsullied by
confrontation,
an acquiescent place
of smooth compliance.

Oh, I can read the blank page
of your guile,
the hieroglyphic
scribbling
in invisible ink
inchoate.

I can understand
your sneering,
your blind assumptions
that your history is
in the future
while my own
never really was.

And
when you talk of talk
in talking you
listen only to yourself.
Silence
opens thoughts where
doors are closed
by noise,
where minds are closed
by certainty –
and you seem so sure
of how the world should work,
of how there must
be no place for
doubt.
In looking back
I see a vapour trail
of multicoloured
laughter –
at the games we played
and lost
(or won),

the losses stacking up
like so many 'so what's
fulcrumed
against wins
uncounted
like so many other 'so what's.

Like so many other 'so what's
we line up the conquests,
the capitulations,
the accords
and treaties broken
like promises.

Like so many other 'so what's
we count the scars
and recall past bruises
reflected in the pooling of
the nightsky blood,
unlit by moons
unlit by stars,
to remind us of the pleasure
to remind us of the pleasure…
the pleasure
of
memory
in the
finger-snap infinity
of
time.

iii

Is there any time left for me now, Auntie Jane?
Is there any time left for me?

Time's up

When the clock without hands,
unaccountably thrown from the window,
strikes thirteen as it lands
on hard times in the street below,
the accordion chimes
of the brokeback clock
will toll, unasked, for us.

Too late to talk it over.

Lest we forget

Another ANZAC day has passed,
attended by a sullen crowd
bovine before a dead wreath monument.
Sanctimonious blathering spoken loud
into the breaking day until, at last,
the posturing done, the righteous went
away, heading home – or better yet –
the pub. Lest we forget.

Every day a songbird dies,
crushed beneath a towering rage
of impotence and accumulated hate.
Somehow, the castle is a rusted cage
in which the battered songbird lies,
the victim of a callous cruel mate
who sees his partner as some tethered pet,
to pamper or to punish – lest she forget.

Each year, men remember men.
They gather in their heroes' bands
to cry pathetic tears, then
they behave as comradeship demands
and tell tall tales that resurrect
the sorry myths of sorry lives – lest they forget.

A woman dies at home each day,
murdered at her partner's hand.
Society turns its head away,
or buries it beneath the sand;
domestic death lacks warlike glory,
lacks Wilfred Owen's 'pro patria mori'.

For men, perhaps it may be said,
'dulce et decorum est'.
Forgotten women, though, are dead
lest you forget the rest.

The New Possibility

I

While we wait, we play chess to fill in the hours of the days.

There is no allegory in our playing the game, none of that psychology flim-flam with substitution theories and dominance role-playing. And neither is it that honourable entertainment of those civilised eastern noblemen of history, played simultaneously on different levels and planes of intellectual sophistication from behind blank smiles. Inscrutable smiles as sinister as whatever lay behind them. No. It is just a game. It is something we do to pass the time while we wait in rooms which stink of cleanliness and bleach, reeking with the disinfectant of conciliation.

Most of us have no knowledge of the game; and those who do have no interest in teaching the rest. And anyway, that's not what it's all about. We don't know how the board should be arranged or in which way the individual pieces are supposed to move – we don't even understand the object of the game. Not that it matters. The chessmen are placed in some agreed formation – which may change from game to game – and are moved over the squares however we decide they should be until the game is over. Sometimes a game might last for weeks depending on how we've agreed to play it. Of course, we dispense with the kings and queens before we start: there seems little point in even playing games with such fraudulent symbols. And we have thrown away those that stand beside the kings and queens for the same reason. We find enough diversion using just the Towers and Horses and little Men.

But that's all part of it really; we have to wait, however long. So that's how the hours of the days are occupied.

One day, the waiting will come to an end. Suddenly, we will be called and we will be ready to answer the call from our positions on opposite sides of the board.

Will we have time to finish the game in progress? Almost certainly not. And there will be no chance of leaving the board in abeyance, to return to it later, because we all know – well, perhaps not all of us, but most of us know – that there will be no need to come back to that particular game: there will be no more waiting.

All we can really hope for, when the call comes, is that one of us will be only a single move away from victory (or defeat) or that a new game has not yet started. Both seem unlikely situations but that is what hope is for: hope challenges the unlikely.

In the meantime, we continue to play with a greater or lesser degree of interest (although never relish, because relish gilds the very pinnacle of involvement, it is the demonstration of an enjoyment which would be totally out of place amongst the arbitrary moves of a simple pastime. No, the enjoyment – and the relishing it – will follow. When the games of chess lie in the tattered disarray of instant abandonment the time for enjoyment, and for the unreserved expression of that enjoyment, will quickly arrive. Time and place, place and time. Like the board itself, black and white, white and black).

II

Black and white...

What colour is the sky outside the room? Sometimes that shade of blue which is green and sometimes that shade of black which is more than black. Sometimes the sky is green-black and swollen where it meets the sea in winter.

White and black…

What colour is the earth beyond the walls? In parts, it is as grey as the dust of annihilation and in parts it lies blackened as by old blood from the wounds of the fallen. Overall the colour of the earth is grey-black and blurred like the eyes of old women sliding into death at dusk.

Black and white…

What colour is the fragrance of the air out in the open? For wave after wave it is baby-shit ochre, the sulphurous colour of smouldering disease. And wave between wave is the green of putrescence so that where the waves swirl and eddy the pustular green-ochre is the slime on the sleeves of tubercular children.

White and black…

What colour is the taste of the water out in the open? The colour of the water which remains tastes of thick tin on the tongue where it still froths in the charred hills. But on the plains, in the stagnant rivers and congealing oceans, the colour is that of hot soap at the back of the throat.

Black and white…

What colour is the victory (or defeat)? There is no victory (and therefore no defeat) because there can be no solution. No resolution. There is only the Mobius strip of continuation which moves in the void, now fast (and colourless) and now slow (and colourless).

III

'The problem is,' she says pointing an index finger heavenwards as though accusing the gods (as if it was all their fault – which maybe it is). 'The problem is, we don't have wars any more. Not proper wars.'

Voices rumble like distant tanks in the night, too far away to identify as hostile or friendly. Lowered heads sway like flowers in some after-blast or impatient wind: affirming, disagreeing, disbelieving, encouraging. And, of course, none of these.

'Oh, we have our minor clashes from time to time.' The index finger has become a hand which waves in airy dismissal. 'And these clashes will doubtless seem important to those who are inconvenienced by them. But they are not wars. Skirmishes, yes; conflicts, yes; battles and massacres and revolutions and uprisings and conflagrations, yes, yes, yes –' swell of voices as the tanks draw nearer but the night is yet dark enough to conceal their colours. 'But war? No. War is…great –' rising swell. In anger? bewilderment? excitement? 'in the sense of being vast and far-reaching and all-encompassing… In the sense of denying all compromise, of calling every one of us. Not these petty fracas which fall more often into the realm of policemen rather than that of the soldier –' heads tremble more violently although eyes (brown green blue yellow grey) remain fixed on the floor – 'the true soldier who is the only one capable of dealing with such monumental responsibility'.

A pause and feet shuffle. But she continues before the pause needs to be filled. 'War is glorious and glory is not an automatic right of anyone. Neither is glory heroism. Everyone has access to heroism. To be heroic one merely has to stand alone. Glory, on the other hand, ah, glory comes from standing together. Heroics are for the stupid, for the undisciplined. And besides, one may be a hero in the civilian sphere. So, heroism has nothing to do with glory. One must learn to ascend to glory through that very discipline that is lacking in the hero. And the demands are such that not everyone has the necessary qualities. Unfortunately. Because glory is inarguably the ultimate triumph in the theatre of war and therefore in life (and death) –' someone close to, leaping up looking about wild-eyed in agitation, tongue-flickering-lips-shine-hands-clasp-unclasp, all heads turning to mute collapse and again sit in bowed and silent confusion 'in the theatre of war where every detail is of vital importance, from crawling on your belly – kitten-crawl, leopard-crawl, monkey-run – until you can stand upright where you belong without shame without shame without –' Briefly she holds her hand to her forehead and frowns. '– to the missile and…to the missile which…which…so to speak…nail…colours to…mast…' Still she holds her hand to her forehead, still she frowns. 'Gas,' she says, looking around, searching for only she knows what. 'Gas and bullets and bayonets and fingernails torn out and warheads and…nuclear warheads…until victory (or defeat). Until the final possibility, the ultimate possibility of glory.' She looks above their heads as if she can see some manifestation of divine power hovering over them in the air (which perhaps she can). 'We are,' she says, 'machines developed by nature to fight-to-protect-to-attack, to eat the meat of those who stand before us and who are too weak themselves to resist us, conquer-us, eat the meat of our destruction. Struggle is our environment, fighting our only choice. Real war is our one true ambition.' Her voice falls in reverence as she bright-eyed stares in challenge.

But the tanks have withdrawn from the assembled throats, have been replaced by the rustling of angels' wings, which are also the sighs of sleeping children.

'The problem is we don't have wars any more.' She points

an index finger heavenwards as though accusing the gods (as if it was all their fault – which maybe it is).

IV

Because there are no more wars, we play chess to fill in the hours of the days while we wait for the call which will tell us that, finally and at last, the greatest of all great wars is about to begin.

What colour is the war? In the beginning, the war was black and white. But now it is all the colours we have come to know and in time it will become all the colours we have yet to name.

Do Not Confuse Life With Illusion

Must we grovel to each other for forgiveness,
licking wounds that really don't exist?

Must our friendship be denied because
you're always sober while I am often pissed?

Endgame #5

The spider I'm afraid of
has your head
between its jaws
and its legs
around
your neck.

I've won.
I've won.

www.ingramcontent.com/pod-product-compliance
Lightning Source LLC
Chambersburg PA
CBHW062149100526
44589CB00014B/1754